A MAGICAL WINTERTIME ON THE FARM

A Magical Wintertime On The Farm

Copyright © 2024 by Jennifer Russell. All rights reserved.

No part of this publication may be reproduced, distributed, or transmitted in any form or by any means, including photocopying, recording, or other electronic or mechanical methods, without the prior written permission of the publisher, except in the case of brief quotations embodied in critical reviews and certain other noncommercial uses permitted by copyright law.

ISBN: 979-8-89316-020-8 (Paperback)
ISBN: 979-8-89316-021-5 (Hardcover)
ISBN: 979-8-89316-022-2 (Ebook)

A Magical Winter time on the Farm

by: Jennifer Russell
Illustrated by: Ian Gonzales

Once upon a time, in a cozy little village, there were a little boy named John and his Uncle Jacob. They were excited because it was that special time of the year when they visited the family's farm to help get everything ready for winter.

One cold morning, Jacob and John put on their warm jackets and colorful scarves, and they set off for the farm. The farm was a magical place, with animals, big red barns, and fields stretching as far as the eye could see.

When they arrived, John's grandma greeted them with a warm smile. She offered the boys warm brownies and milk. She had a twinkle in her eye as she handed the boys a basket of apples and table scraps. "It's time to prepare for winter, and we need your help," she said.

The boys knew exactly what to do. They headed to the barn to feed the animals. The cows, chickens, and donkeys were all eager for their tasty treats. Jacob and John giggled as they watched the animals munch on the delicious food.

After the animals were fed, John's grandpa showed them how to stack hay in the barn to keep it warm for the animals during the cold winter. The boys worked hard, piling up the golden hay bales one by one. They imagined the animals snuggling up in the soft hay, safe and warm.

As the day went on, the boys gathered firewood for the farmhouse's cozy fireplace. They knew that the warm fire would keep them all toasty during the cold winter nights.

Finally, as the sun began to set, the family gathered around the farmhouse table for a delicious dinner. Before they ate, they held hands, and John's grandpa led a special prayer. "Dear Lord, we thank you for this bountiful harvest and for the safety and well-being of our animals during the winter ahead. Please watch over them and keep them warm and healthy. Amen."

Jacob and John listened with reverence, feeling a deep sense of connection to the farm and its animals. They knew that the farm was not just a place where they played and worked but a place filled with love and care for all its creatures.

As they finished their meal, the family sat by the crackling fireplace, sharing stories and laughter. The boys were so grateful for this special day, and they drifted off to sleep with dreams of happy animals nestled in their warm barn.

The next morning, Jacob and John woke up to the sound of roosters crowing. They knew they had to say goodbye to the farm and head back home. As they left, they promised to visit again soon and help prepare for the next winter.

The two boys held each other's hands and John whispered a little prayer of his own for the animals. "Dear Lord, please keep the farm animals safe and warm this winter, just like my grandparents do. Amen."

With their hearts full of love and hope, Jacob and John waved goodbye to the farm, knowing that they had done their part to care for the animals and that the farm would always be a place of warmth and love, no matter how cold the winter might become.

www.ingramcontent.com/pod-product-compliance
Lightning Source LLC
Chambersburg PA
CBHW061350010526
44107CB00011B/893